D1708884

Inside
AMERICAN POLITICS

Supreme Court
Decisions

By Anita Croy

LUCENT
PRESS

Published in 2019 by
Lucent Press, an Imprint of Greenhaven Publishing, LLC
353 3rd Avenue
Suite 255
New York, NY 10010

For Brown Bear Books Ltd
Editorial Director: Lindsey Lowe
Managing Editor: Tim Cooke
Designer: Lynne Lennon
Design Manager: Keith Davis
Picture Manager: Sophie Mortimer
Children's Publisher: Anne O'Daly

Picture Credits
Front cover: Eric Thayer/Getty Images News/Getty Images
Interior: Alamy: Ian Dagnall Computing, 18; **iStock:** 400tmax, 24, Joe Belanger, 43, Joel Carillet, 44,
Steve Debenport, 25, DK Fielding, 4, 5, SolStock, 38; **Library of Congress:** 10, 15, 30, 31; **Open Access:**
U.S. Government Elections/TopCat, 22, wlrn.org, 37; **Public Domain:** National Archives and Records
Administration, 8, National Portrait Gallery of Eminent Americans/The Cooper Collection/Centpacrr, 14,
New York Times, 23, Lorie Shaull, 19, collection of the Supreme Court of the United States/Franz Jantzen,
34, collection of the Supreme Court of the United States/Steve Petteway, 7, 13, U.S. Army, 17, U.S. Federal
Government/Ollie Atkins, 20, U. S. Government/Department of Homeland Security/Gerald L. Nino, CBP, 18,
United States Government, 45; **Shutterstock:** BoxerX, 21, CRATISTA, 26, Everett Historical, 9, 36, 42, Sheila
Fitzgerald, 33, John Gomez, 32, Inspired by Maps, 27, KMH Photovideo, 39, Timur Laykov, 40, Lee Snider
Photo Images, 6, Rena Schild, 11, Sean Locke Photography, 41, George Sheldon, 28, SNEHIT, 35, Joseph
Sohm, 29, Stock Photo World, 12.

Brown Bear Books has made every attempt to contact the copyright holders.
If you have any information please contact licensing@brownbearbooks.co.uk

Cataloging-in-Publication Data

Names: Croy, Anita.
Title: Supreme court decisions / Anita Croy.
Description: New York : Lucent Press, 2019. | Series: Inside American politics | Includes glossary and index.
Identifiers: ISBN 9781534566743 (pbk.) | ISBN 9781534566750 (library bound) |
ISBN 9781534566767 (ebook)
Subjects: LCSH: United States. Supreme Court–Juvenile literature. | United States. Supreme Court–Rules and
practice–Juvenile literature. | Law–United States–Juvenile literature.
Classification: LCC KF8742.C79 2019 | DDC 347.73'26–dc23

Printed in the United States of America

CPSIA compliance information: Batch #BW19KL: For further information contact Greenhaven Publishing LLC, New York, New York at 1-844-317-7404.

Please visit our website, www.greenhavenpublishing.com. For a free color catalog of all our
high-quality books, call toll free 1-844-317-7404 or fax 1-844-317-7405.

Contents

Chapter 1

THE ULTIMATE COURT

The Supreme Court is the highest legal authority in the United States. Its task is to review US laws to make sure they conform to the Constitution. The court's decisions are absolute and final, and can only be overturned by the court itself. Every court in the country, from local courts to federal **circuit courts**, must follow any ruling made by the Supreme Court. The nine justices on the court hold their positions for life—that places them among the most influential officials in the nation.

The US Supreme Court Building near Capitol Hill in Washington, D.C., was built between 1932 and 1935 to house the Supreme Court. The court had previously sat in the Capitol itself.

Every year, lower courts send thousands of rulings to the Supreme Court for review. Of those, the court considers about 100 cases. It decides whether federal, state, or local governments are acting within the law. Each justice has one vote and all nine justices must vote, so every ruling must be approved by at least 5 votes to 4.

The Supreme Court is laid out like other courtrooms, with the justices facing the desks of lawyers and other witnesses.

A Job for Life

Only the president can nominate a judge to the Supreme Court. The nomination then has to be approved by the Senate. The opportunity to appoint a new justice is rare, and some presidents do not get to nominate a justice. In the past, senators assessed new justices on their qualifications, character, and past actions. In recent years, they more often appoint justices who reflect their own political beliefs.

In 1986, Republican President Ronald Reagan nominated the **conservative** Antonin Scalia to the Supreme Court. The Senate approved Scalia by 98 votes to 0. In contrast, when President Donald Trump nominated Judge Neil Gorsuch in 2017, the nomination was highly controversial.

Inscribed on the front of the Supreme Court Building in Washington, D.C., is the motto, "Equal justice under law." The phrase is not in the Constitution, but is based on a Supreme Court judgment in 1891. The idea comes from ancient Greece, where in 431 BC the Athenian leader Pericles described how justice should work. Translated from Greek into English, his words have been interpreted to mean that everyone—irrespective of their social position, profession, or wealth—is entitled to be treated the same in a court of law.

The Supreme Court Building was constructed in a neoclassical style to underline its importance in US life. One justice complained that the new building was "pretentious."

Trump's predecessor, President Barack Obama, had nominated a moderate judge, Merrick Garland, but Republican senators delayed approving Garland until the 2016 presidential election, when Obama's nomination lapsed. One of Trump's first actions as president was to nominate Neil Gorsuch for the vacant position.

Antonin Scalia was an associate justice from 1986 until his death in 2016. Republicans deliberately delayed approving his successor.

The Republican majority in the Senate approved his nomination by using the so-called **nuclear option**, which requires only a simple majority. Gorsuch was approved by 54 votes to 45. Some observers believed that Gorsuch's appointment was more influenced by his politics than by his legal expertise.

WHAT DO YOU THINK?

Republican senators delayed Barack Obama's nominee for the seat on the Supreme Court in the hopes of nominating a more conservative judge. In what ways might they have been forced to act sooner?

Chapter 2

WHAT IS THE
SUPREME COURT?

The US Constitution created the Supreme Court as one of the three branches of government. The other branches are the legislative and executive branches. The legislative branch, or Congress—the Senate and the House of Representatives—makes new laws. The executive branch is led by the president and implements the laws. The Supreme Court reviews laws made by Congress and judges the constitutionality of executive actions.

Court of Last Resort

The Supreme Court is the highest court in the land. Before a case reaches the Supreme Court, it has passed through the state

The Constitution created the Supreme Court but did not explicitly describe its powers.

or federal court system. It can take many years for a case to reach the Supreme Court. Each time a case is heard, the lower court's decision must be appealed, so the case moves on to a higher court. There are exceptions, such as cases that involve **diplomats** from other countries. The Supreme Court is the final step in the legal process. It is the court of last resort.

The Supreme Court decides which cases to hear from up to 10,000 put forward for review each year. In recent decades, the number of cases the court hears has been about 100 a year. If the court does not choose to review a case, the ruling of the lower court stands.

Making Decisions

The senior justice of the Supreme Court is the Chief Justice, who is nominated by the president and confirmed by the

William Howard Taft, who was Chief Justice from 1921 to 1930, had previously served as US president.

Senate. The Chief Justice makes a list of cases for review. The other eight justices may also add cases to the list, and the justices discuss which cases to accept. The "Rule of Four" means that if four justices agree to review a case the review goes ahead.

A Supreme Court ruling led to the integration of US public schools, so black and white students could learn together.

The justices usually review cases that affect the whole country or a particular part of society. In 1954, for example, the Supreme Court reviewed *Browns v. Board of Education.* A group of Kansas parents had taken the state to court over its policy of racial **segregation**. At the time, there was widespread debate about civil rights. When the Supreme Court ruled in favor of the parents, the decision put an end to racial segregation not just in Kansas, but in the entire public school system.

The Court at Work

The Supreme Court sits from the first Monday in October until June or July the following year. It works on an

---

WHAT DO YOU THINK?

A Supreme Court justice is appointed for life or until he or she decides to retire. What advantages can you think of that might be gained from allowing justices to serve unlimited terms?

THE POWER OF THE PEOPLE

The Supreme Court is supposed to be nonpolitical. The chief justice and the associate justices are unelected government officials. Because justices are chosen by the president, however, their appointment often reflects political considerations. Legal scholars suggest that presidents increasingly pay attention to public opinion when nominating a judge for Senate confirmation. The president tries to identify a justice who will interpret constitutional issues in a particular way that reflects the wishes of his own supporters.

A sign against same-sex marriage outside the Supreme Court in June 2016. Such protests reflect the growing politicization of the court's decisions.

alternating two-week cycle of "sittings" and "recesses." During a two-week sitting, the justices hear cases. They listen to opposing lawyers making their cases, and are able to interrupt and ask as many questions as they want. Often, justices hear details of more than one case in a day.

The courtroom contains nine chairs for the justices, all of whom must be present during a case.

During the two-week recess, the justices sit in a locked room to discuss the case and write up their legal opinions before voting. One of the justices for the majority in the case writes a majority opinion explaining the decision. If judges in the minority strongly disagree with the decision of their colleagues, they can write a dissenting minority opinion.

Who's Who

The Constitution does not specify the number of justices on the Supreme Court. There have been as few as six and as many as ten. Today, there are nine. They do not have to be judges or lawyers, but the majority are. Since the first US government was established, more than 100 men have served on the Supreme Court. The first African American justice was Thurgood Marshall, appointed in 1967. In 1981, Sandra Day O'Connor became the first woman associate justice. In 2018, there were three women serving as associate justices on the Supreme Court: Ruth Bader Ginsburg, who was appointed by President Clinton in 1993, Sonia Sotomayor, and Elena Kagan, both appointed by President Obama in 2009 and 2010, respectively.

The first four female justices on the Supreme Court: (left to right) Sandra Day O'Connor, Sonia Sotomayor, Ruth Bader Ginsburg, and Elena Kagan.

WHAT DO YOU THINK?

There is currently an odd number of justices, so there is always a majority. In the past, however, there has been an even number. In that case, how might they reach a conclusion in the event of a tied decision?

Chapter 3

THE SUPREME COURT
IN HISTORY

Since independence, the decisions of the Supreme Court have had a profound impact on American life. It has judged many issues about what kind of society America should become, from the rights of African Americans and women to the procedure for arresting criminals.

John Marshall studied law for only six weeks, but spent 34 years as Chief Justice.

Setting a Precedent

The original Supreme Court was so unimportant that the planners of Washington, D.C., forgot to build a place for it to meet. That changed in 1801, when John Marshall became chief justice. Marshall would establish the court's prominence in the government.

In 1803, the court reviewed the *Marbury v. Madison* case. William Marbury had been appointed as a justice of the peace by the outgoing president, John Adams.

However, the government had changed, and the new Secretary of State, James Madison, overturned Marbury's appointment. Marbury asked the Supreme Court to honor it, and although the court agreed with his right to claim the post, it ruled that the act of Congress under which he had that right was unconstitutional. This meant that the court could not help Marbury. However, the ruling established the Supreme Court's power of judicial review. It confirmed that the court could overturn the decisions of Congress if it believed they did not stick to the Constitution.

Slavery and Race

One area in which the Supreme Court has had great influence has been in **civil rights**—but not always in a positive way. In 1857, for example, the court ruled in the case of *Dred Scott v. Sandford*. Ten years earlier, slaves Dred and Harriet Scott, had **sued** for their freedom after living for some time with their owner in the free territory of Wisconsin. The Supreme Court ruled

The court's ruling that Dred and Harriet Scott had no rights angered antislavery campaigners.

Public transportation was racially segregated until the 1950s under the principle of "separate but equal." However, black facilities were rarely equal to those provided for white citizens.

that, as slaves, the Scotts were not citizens of the United States. That meant they were not protected by the US Constitution, and so had no right to appeal to the legal system. The issue of African American rights continued after the Civil War (1861–1865) and the emancipation of the slaves in 1863.

In 1896, the case of *Plessy v. Ferguson* was brought before the Supreme Court by Homer Plessy, who was one-eighth African American. Plessy had a first-class ticket for a train in Louisiana.

WHAT DO YOU THINK?

Many of the people who wrote and ratified the Constitution owned slaves. How might knowing that affect how we interpret its provisions today?

However, under the Separate Car Law, he was arrested for trying to sit in the first-class carriage, as white and African Americans had to sit in separate train carriages. The Supreme Court ruled that Plessy's arrest was fair. This supported the system of segregation set up under so-called **Jim Crow laws** in which black Americans were entitled to "separate but equal" facilities compared to white Americans.

In 1954, the Supreme Court overturned *Plessy v. Ferguson* and ruled that segregation was unconstitutional. In *Brown v. the Board of Education*, the justices unanimously ruled that it was wrong for third-grader Linda Brown to have to travel to a black school when there was a white school much closer to her home. The ruling implied that Americans could no longer be **discriminated** against because of their color, although it took another decade for this to become the law.

US paratroopers escort black children into Little Rock High School in Arkansas when it was forcibly integrated in 1957.

The Justice System

The modern US justice system owes two of its fundamental rights to the Supreme Court. In 1963, a small-time criminal named Clarence Earl Gideon was put on trial in Florida. Gideon could not afford a lawyer, so he had to defend himself in court. He lost his case and was sent to jail. He sued Florida's Divisions of Corrections, arguing that he had been denied a fair trial. The Supreme Court agreed that his Fourteenth Amendment

A US border agent reads a suspect his rights, a process known as "mirandizing" for the Supreme Court case of 1963.

right to equal protection under the law had been violated. Since then, every defendant has the right to legal representation, regardless of their ability to pay. Three years later, in *Miranda v. Arizona* (1963), the Supreme Court ruled that the police must advise prisoners of their legal rights before being arrested and questioned.

WHAT DO YOU THINK?

TV shows and movies mean that everyone is familiar with the Miranda rights, such as "You have the right to remain silent." How do these rights help to prevent miscarriages of justice?

Women's Rights

In 1973, in a landmark ruling known as *Roe v. Wade*, the Supreme Court agreed with a Texas woman known as "Jane Roe" that she should be allowed to decide for herself whether to continue with her pregnancy. At the time, **abortion** was illegal in Texas. The ruling made abortion legal in all 50 states. It remains one of the most controversial of all US laws. In 2016, the question came before the Supreme Court again. The court ruled that a woman was free to seek an abortion in *Whole Women's Health v. Hellerstedt*.

Other Rulings

In 1964, the Supreme Court ruled on press reporting. The police commissioner of Montgomery, Alabama, L. B. Sullivan, sued the *New York Times* and four religious ministers for **libel**. Sullivan said he had been defamed by an advertisement the ministers placed in the paper about the arrest of the civil rights leader, Martin Luther King, Jr.

Jane Roe, whose real name was Norma McCorvey (left), was a single woman who did not want to continue with her third pregnancy.

Sullivan had been awarded **damages** in the lower courts, but the *New York Times* appealed. The Supreme Court ruled against Sullivan. It argued that the First Amendment protecting free speech protects press reports about public officials provided they are made without malice.

In 1974, the Supreme Court made another landmark ruling. This time it ruled that a president cannot use executive privilege to withhold evidence during a trial. During what is

Richard Nixon waves from his helicopter as he gives up the presidency in 1974.

known as the Watergate scandal, President Richard Nixon withheld evidence of how much he knew about a criminal conspiracy. In *United States v. Nixon*, the court ruled that Nixon had to hand the evidence to a federal court.

WHAT DO YOU THINK?

President Nixon argued that a president's executive privileges mean they should be treated differently than other citizens under law. How does this fit with the ideal of "Equal justice under law"?

THE POWER OF THE PEOPLE

In the 1970s, a white Californian named Allan Bakke had his application for medical school turned down twice. In 1978, Bakke sued the University of California. He argued that his grades were better than those of ethnic minority students who had been admitted. The justices ruled that Bakke should be admitted, but also that institutions were able to practice **affirmative action**. This meant they could favor minority candidates for education or jobs to try to increase social opportunity.

Allan Bakke was finally admitted to the School of Medicine at the University of California, Davis, to train as a doctor, but the university was ruled to have acted legally in excluding him.

Chapter 4

THE SUPREME COURT TODAY

Since the start of the 2000s, politics in Washington has become more **polarized** between the two main political parties. The Supreme Court has been asked to rule on contentious issues that divide the US public, such as the Second Amendment right to bear arms.

Election Contest

In November 2000, the presidential election between Republican George W. Bush and Democrat Al Gore came down to one state. The result in Florida would decide the overall result. Electronic counts gave the candidates almost the same number of votes, so courts ordered a recount to check for mistakes.

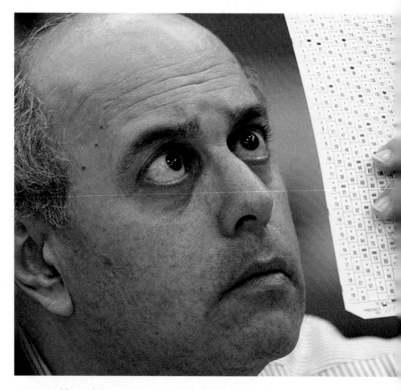

An official examines a ballot paper during a manual recount in Florida after the 2000 presidential election.

"All the News That's Fit to Print"

The New York Times

Late Edition
New York: Today, bright start, then cloudy, high 31. Tonight, snow arriving, low 28. Tomorrow, snow changing to rain, high 35. Yesterday, high 52, low 37. Weather map is on Page D8.

VOL. CL.... No. 51,601   Copyright © 2000 The New York Times   NEW YORK, WEDNESDAY, DECEMBER 13, 2000 $1 beyond the greater New York metropolitan area.   75 CENTS

Bush Prevails as Justices, 5-4, End Recounting

Another Part of the Battle: Keeping a Drug in the Store

By JEFF GERTH and SHERYL GAY STOLBERG

MEDICINE MERCHANTS
When Regulators Say No

Odell Buggs walked into the federal courthouse in downtown Rochester on a cold and snowy Tuesday in December 1999, not knowing quite what to expect. She walked out with a promise from one of the world's biggest pharmaceutical manufacturers to pay her $1.3 million.

Six years earlier, Ms. Buggs, then a 26-year-old counselor for needy children, had suffered a stroke that her doctors attributed to an ingredient in her over-the-counter decongestant, Tavist-D. She sued the manufacturer, the pharmaceutical giant Novartis A.G., saying its cold pill had left her with brain damage.

Novartis, based in Switzerland, had a strong defense: the ingredient, phenylpropanolamine, or PPA, was in dozens of cold remedies, as well as appetite suppressants, and had been taken in billions of doses with no ill effects.

But by the time Ms. Buggs arrived in court, Novartis knew something the public did not: Yale University researchers had tentatively concluded that PPA was linked to a slight risk of stroke in young women. The company offered to settle, and Ms. Buggs accepted. But there was a

Drug companies protested, saying that the Yale scientists were wrong and that the drug was safe. But nonetheless, they removed the products from store shelves. Ms. Buggs was elated. "Now," she said, "people will see."

The Buggs case offers a glimpse into how companies marketing PPA worked aggressively to assuage concerns about the safety of a drug that for six decades was a staple in American medicine cabinets. It also sheds light on a larger issue: pharmaceutical companies, which spend more than $20 billion a year researching and developing medicines, devote far less attention to examining how their drugs are used by consumers.

In the case of PPA, safety questions simmered for two decades on three fronts: in scientific circles, the courts and in Washington. In each arena, an examination of court records and other documents shows, pharmaceutical companies or their representatives tried to tamp down the public debate.

In scientific circles, a university pharmacologist acted as a re-

Thirty-five days after Election Day, Gov. George W. Bush won a major victory in the Supreme Court.

Associated Press

Putin Nurturing Old Friendships

Hundreds Waiting in Florida Spent Day in State of Limbo

UNSIGNED OPINION

Ruling Effectively Gives Election Victory to Governor of Texas

By LINDA GREENHOUSE

WASHINGTON, Dec. 12 — The Supreme Court effectively handed the presidential election to George W. Bush tonight, overturning the Florida Supreme Court and ruling by a vote of 5 to 4 that there could be no further counting of Florida's disputed presidential votes.

The ruling came after a long and tense day of waiting at 10 p.m., just two hours before the Dec. 12 "safe harbor" for immunizing a state's electors from challenge in Congress was to come to an end. The unsigned majority opinion said it was the immediacy of this deadline that made it impossible to come up with a way of counting the votes that could both meet "minimal constitutional standards" and be accomplished within the deadline.

The five members of the majority were Chief Justice William H. Rehnquist and Justices Sandra Day O'Connor, Antonin Scalia, Anthony M. Kennedy and Clarence Thomas. Among the four dissenters, two justices, Stephen G. Breyer and Da-

A newspaper headline reflects the decision in the Supreme Court over the 2000 election result, which was decided 5 votes to 4.

When the number of votes between the two candidates shrank still further, the courts ordered more recounts. As the election dragged into December, George W. Bush appealed to the Supreme Court to stop the recounts and rule him the victor.

The Supreme Court agreed with Bush's argument that it was impossible to complete another manual recount in an appropriate amount of time. A month after the actual election, George W. Bush was declared the 43th president of the United States. For many people, the Supreme Court's involvement had not settled the question of whether George W. Bush had won a fair victory. Many people complained that the Supreme Court had been used as a political tool rather than as a court of last resort.

Gun Control

The question of whether there should be tighter gun ownership laws has become an important issue in recent years because of an increase in deadly shootings across the country. The Supreme Court considered *District of Columbia v. Heller* in 2008. The District of Columbia had banned citizens from keeping firearms at home for self-defense. The court ruled that the Second Amendment protects a citizen's right to keep a firearm. For the pro-gun lobby, the ruling remains proof that gun ownership is enshrined in the US Constitution and cannot be challenged.

In 2017, about 42 percent of US households owned at least one gun. At its peak, in 1990, gun ownership was at 47 percent.

Health Care

Another contentious issue in modern America is how to pay for medical care. Millions of Americans cannot afford health care insurance. President Bill Clinton tried to introduce an affordable health care program during his presidency in the 1990s and failed. President Barack Obama made affordable health care for everyone one of the key pledges of his presidency, and the Affordable Care Act (ACA) was enacted in 2010. It required all Americans to have health insurance or pay a penalty.

The ACA, or Obamacare, was highly controversial. The Supreme Court ruled on the debate in 2012, after the National Federation of Independent Business took the government to court over the reforms. The court upheld the ACA. Its ruling forced businesses of any size to give their employees access to health insurance. The ACA was at the center of another Supreme Court ruling in 2015. The justices considered how to interpret the act and whether the ruling applied equally to all 50 states.

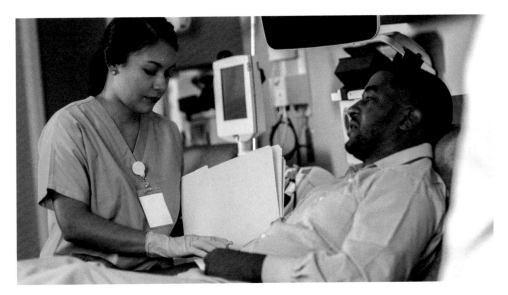

Before the ACA, about 48 million Americans were without medical insurance. In 2016, under ACA, the number had fallen to about 28 million.

WHAT DO YOU THINK?

As the Supreme Court becomes politicized, it comes under more pressure to review previous judgments on controversial issues. How might it be possible to decide that an issue is resolved once and for all?

In *King et al v. Burwell, Secretary of Health and Human Services, et al* (2015), the Supreme Court ruled that federal tax credits for health care must be available in every state, even if a state had its own health care provision for its citizens.

Massachusetts was the first US state to allow same-sex marriages, in 2004.

Same-Sex Marriage

In 2013, the Supreme Court in *United States v. Windsor* redefined what marriage meant in America. The 1996 Defense of Marriage Act had defined marriage as a legally binding union between a man and a woman. A woman named Edith Windsor lived in New York State with her wife, Thea Spyer, whom she had married in Canada. When Spyer died, Windsor found that she did not qualify for federal tax exemption on inheriting Spyer's **estate** because the federal government did not recognize their marriage.

WHAT DO YOU THINK?

Some states had recognized same-sex marriages for up to nine years before the Supreme Court ruled on the issue. Is that too long a delay? If so, what could be done to speed up the process?

The Supreme Court ruled that the definitions in the Defense of Marriage Act failed to protect the rights of same-sex married couples, as set out in the Fifth Amendment. Following the ruling, the federal government was bound to offer the same benefits to legally married same-sex couples as to heterosexual married couples.

The Race Question

The question of race also continues to split opinion across the nation since the passing of civil rights legislation in the 1960s. In 2016, Abigail Fisher sued the University of Texas after the university rejected her application to become a student. Fisher argued that she had been discriminated against because she was white. She said that her grades were better than those of many African-American students who had been admitted because of their color. The Supreme Court upheld the university's decision. The decision effectively ruled that affirmative action was constitutional.

Abigail Fisher's case against the University of Texas was similar to the Allan Bakke case of 1978.

Legal Challenges

After Donald Trump became president in January 2017, he imposed a ban on travelers from seven mainly Muslim countries. The ban was overturned in the courts as being unconstitutional. In December, a revised version of the ban went into effect. It faced legal challenges, however, but it was ultimately upheld by the Supreme Court in June 2018.

Donald Trump's supporters widely approved of his travel ban, which the Supreme Court upheld in 2018, although other Americans protested the ban.

WHAT DO YOU THINK?

The Supreme Court decided at first to allow the travel ban to take effect while its legality was considered in the courts. How might this be preferable to not allowing it to come into effect until a decision was made?

NOVEMBER 12th
Mobilize
FOR
WOMEN'S
LIVES
ACROSS THE USA & WASHINGTON, DC

THE POWER OF THE PEOPLE

A Supreme Court ruling does not always end debate on an issue. In *Roe v. Wade* (1973), the court ruled that it was unconstitutional to ban abortion, but the question continues to divide opinion. Courts in some states, such as Texas, have passed laws to make having an abortion more difficult. In response, women who support the pro-choice movement have spent decades protesting and marching to support the right to easily available abortion. Both pro-choice and pro-life campaigners remain highly visible and highly vocal in an effort to keep the issue in the public arena.

A demonstration outside the state capitol in Jefferson City, Missouri, in support of the right of women to choose whether or not to have an abortion.

NARAL
National Abortion Rights Action League

CONTROVERSIES AND DEBATES

As the most senior court in the land, the Supreme Court ensures that the US Constitution is upheld. The laws are open to interpretation, however, and many of the court's rulings have been controversial. In recent years, particularly, the Supreme Court has found itself being asked to referee between opposing political views.

Scandals

The only qualification the Constitution requires for a Supreme Court justice is "good behavior." Justices are meant to defend the Constitution and the

James Clark McReynolds had served as attorney general before becoming an associate justice.

primacy of the law even when that means acting against their own opinions. However, some justices have displayed questionable behavior. In 1914, for example, President Woodrow Wilson nominated James Clark McReynolds of Tennessee to the court.

McReynolds was by all accounts too lazy to read his case notes carefully and was known for bullying his staff. He was also anti-Semitic in his views and refused to speak to his fellow associate justice Louis Brandeis for three years because Brandeis was Jewish.

Hugo Lafayette Black was a former senator from Alabama who became a Justice in 1937.

Hugo Lafayette Black, meanwhile, was made a justice by President Franklin D. Roosevelt. Black was a former member of the Ku Klux Klan. However, as a supporter of the Constitution, Black continued to serve on the Supreme Court for more than 30 years.

Controversial Decisions

Throughout history, the most controversial Supreme Court decisions have involved issues that bitterly divide Americans. In the 1800s, these included issues such as slavery. In the 1900s, the court's rulings on New Deal legislation during the Great Depression and on civil rights in the 1950s and 1960s were also highly contentious. Controversial subjects such as abortion rights and gun control continue to be live issues in US politics.

Supreme Court decisions often attract scrutiny and protest around the world, including in London, England.

Dealing with Immigration

Some critics say that the Supreme Court has become too closely involved in political debate. One example is the debate over immigration. President Barack Obama, for example, introduced the Deferred Action for Childhood Arrivals (DACA) program in 2012. The program addressed the status of around 800,000 "Dreamers." These were immigrant children who came to the United States illegally and would soon be eligible for deportation. DACA allowed the students to avoid deportation and made them eligible for a work permit.

Critics believe DACA encourages illegal immigration. President Donald Trump came to office committed to ending the program. His Attorney General, Jeff Sessions, asked the Supreme Court to declare DACA unconstitutional. Sessions and the Department of Justice argued that Barack Obama had overreached his presidential power to create the program.

Opponents of the administration claimed that the Attorney General cannot petition the Supreme Court, so Sessions was misusing his power. Many legal observers believed that the administration was trying to force the court to make the decision it wanted. By appealing directly to the Supreme Court, critics argued, the administration ignored **due process**, by which the case would be first tried in the lower courts. In the end, the Supreme Court declined to become involved because those previous trials had not taken place.

President Trump's call to end DACA caused a wave of protests, although he argued that the program itself was illegal.

WHAT DO YOU THINK?

The Constitution gives the Supreme Court the right to stand up to the wishes of the president. The president is elected, however, while the justices are not. How does that strengthen or weaken US democracy?

More controversy surrounded President Trump's first nomination of a justice. The position had become vacant under President Barack Obama, but Republicans in the Senate had deliberately delayed appointing Obama's nominee until after the presidential election in 2016. The new president nominated a conservative justice, Neil Gorsuch, who seemed to share many of Trump's own views. The appointment was approved by the Senate in April 2017.

Neil Gorsuch takes the oath on a Bible held by his wife, Marie, on April 8, 2017. He had previously been a judge in the Court of Appeals for the Tenth Circuit.

WHAT DO YOU THINK?

In the past, justices nominated by presidents were often confirmed unanimously by the Senate. In what ways might Senate battles over nominations weaken the status of the justices, if at all?

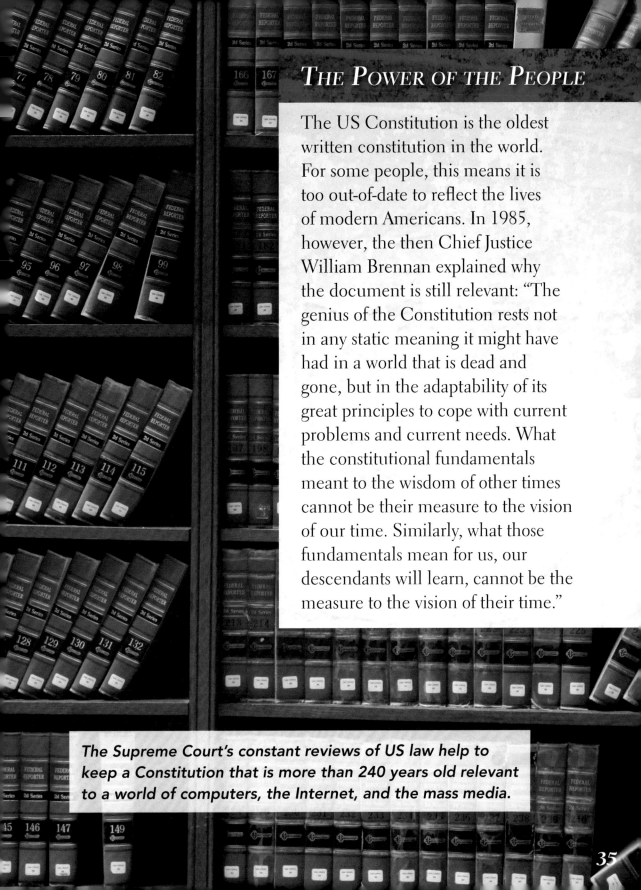

THE POWER OF THE PEOPLE

The US Constitution is the oldest written constitution in the world. For some people, this means it is too out-of-date to reflect the lives of modern Americans. In 1985, however, the then Chief Justice William Brennan explained why the document is still relevant: "The genius of the Constitution rests not in any static meaning it might have had in a world that is dead and gone, but in the adaptability of its great principles to cope with current problems and current needs. What the constitutional fundamentals meant to the wisdom of other times cannot be their measure to the vision of our time. Similarly, what those fundamentals mean for us, our descendants will learn, cannot be the measure to the vision of their time."

The Supreme Court's constant reviews of US law help to keep a Constitution that is more than 240 years old relevant to a world of computers, the Internet, and the mass media.

Chapter 6

THE SUPREME COURT
AND YOU

The Supreme Court affects the everyday lives of every American. Its past rulings have created the modern nation and the modern interpretation of the Constitution guarantees of justice, welfare, and liberty for citizens. The court's rulings today continue to shape the country in which American citizens live. The Supreme Court has changed over time to reflect changing social values, and it is still changing.

In the early years of the Supreme Court, the justices reflected the widespread opinion of the time that slavery was legal under the Constitution and that slaves did not count as full citizens.

In the middle of the 1800s, for example, the court upheld a ruling that African-American slaves were not full citizens. A century later, it ruled that it was unconstitutional to segregate public school children on the basis of race. The ruling paved the way for the civil rights movement of the 1960s, which finally led to racial equality. In 1973, the court ruled that women were in charge of their own bodies and could choose to end an unwanted pregnancy.

Freedom to Vote

One of the Supreme Court's most important jobs is to protect the freedoms the Constitution gives to all citizens. When they turn 18, for example, every American becomes entitled to vote in official elections. However, the Supreme Court has frequently been asked to rule whether that right can be removed in some circumstances, such as if a person has been convicted of a serious felony.

Voters wait in line on election day. The Fifteenth Amendment guaranteed all male citizens the right to vote in 1870, regardless of race or color. Women received the vote in 1920.

In some states, felons who have committed serious crimes lose their right to vote while they are in jail or on parole or probation. In 1974, the Supreme Court had ruled that the Constitution allowed the withdrawal of the right to vote. This ruling was known as felony disenfranchisement. However, the court overturned it in 1985, opening the way for some states to restore the vote to convicted criminals.

Freedom to Marry for Love

In 2015, the Supreme Court ruled that marriage was no longer to be legally understood as a contract only between men and women. Since then, it has been legal to marry a person of the same sex in any US state. This was a huge step for gay rights, as it gave same-sex couples the same rights as other couples and recognized them in federal law.

Same-sex marriage was legal in 36 states before the court's ruling in 2015.

Freedom to Bear Arms

After school shootings in Florida and Texas, many citizens marched to call for a renewed review of America's gun-control laws.

In *District of Columbia v. Heller* (2008), the Supreme Court had ruled that the Constitution protected an individual's right to bear arms. To the disappointment of antigun campaigners, the Supreme Court has not since selected any cases for review that might allow it to revisit this ruling. In the absence of a new ruling, lower courts in each state set their own gun legislation. Some states have imposed limited controls, such as ruling that a firearm must be visible if it is carried, but there has been no serious reform.

In 2018, high school students participated at the "Never Again" rally to protest and change gun laws after the shooting at Marjory Stoneman Douglas High School.

WHAT DO YOU THINK?

Only the justices themselves can decide what cases the Supreme Court reviews. If the court does not take on an issue such as gun control, how might the public's wishes for a review be taken into account?

What is or is not permitted in school has been reviewed by the Supreme Court numerous times.

School Life

Some of the rules that govern how schools operate are the result of Supreme Court rulings. The biggest shake-up was the ending of racial segregation in 1954, but since then the Supreme Court has also ruled on other laws that affect all students. In 1969, for example, it ruled that students had the right to hold protests at school, as guaranteed by the First Amendment, but added that this right must be balanced against a school's need to keep order. In 1971, the court upheld the busing of students to schools to achieve racial integregation. In 1995, the court ruled that random drug tests do not compromise a student's right to privacy, so were permissible.

— WHAT DO YOU THINK? —

Some schools search or scan students as they enter the campus. How can a student's right to privacy be balanced with the school's responsibility to guarantee the safety of all its students?

THE POWER OF THE PEOPLE

Many people believe the idea of the teenager was born with rock 'n' roll in the 1950s. However, there is an argument that the Supreme Court created the teenager with a landmark ruling in 1967 after the arrest of a 15-year-old boy in Arizona. *In re Gault* ("In reference to Gault"), the court ruled for the first time that teenagers have distinct rights under the Constitution. Previously, teenagers had been seen as children who were the property of their parents, who were legally responsible for them and their actions.

In re Gault, *the Supreme Court ruled that juveniles were entitled to the same rights as adults in law, such as being informed of the details of any charges made against them.*

Chapter 7

GETTING INVOLVED

It might appear that individual citizens have little direct connection with the nine justices sitting in the Supreme Court in Washington, DC. In some ways, this is true. Justices are appointed by the president, rather than being elected by voters. Their decisions are not open to public debate and they do not have to pay attention to public opinion. Yet the Supreme Court is part of the same political system as the executive and the legislative branches.

George Washington arrives for his second inauguration in 1793. As the first president, Washington appointed the entire Supreme Court. In all, he appointed a record 10 justices.

By voting for representatives at a local or state level, or in a presidential election, all Americans can help shape the future direction of the country.

Cast Your Vote

The most important way an individual can influence the Supreme Court is through elections. Voting gives all citizens a say in how the United States develops. This can directly affect the makeup of the Supreme Court. Donald Trump's nomination of Neil Gorsuch as justice in 2017, for example, reflected the conservative mood of the country. Trump selected a justice whose ideals would appeal to the voters who put him in the White House. Gorsuch favored the right to life over abortion and opposed increased gun control.

The best way to try to change the makeup of the Supreme Court is to vote for a president who is more or less conservative or liberal. Most presidents get a chance to nominate at least one Supreme Court justice, and they are likely to select someone who reflects their own views.

If you feel strongly about issues that are likely to be addressed by the Supreme Court, write your senators or House members to express your opinions. The court can only consider laws put before it—and it is Congress that makes the laws. To start the debate, therefore, voters need to let Congress know what kinds of laws they want.

Elections can directly influence the makeup of the Supreme Court—and the direction of its future decisions.

Unchanging Tradition

While the political makeup of the Supreme Court changes over time and its future rulings are unknown, one aspect of its role will never change. It will continue to be the highest court in the land, the court of last resort, and the ultimate protector of the US Constitution.

WHAT DO YOU THINK?

In theory anyone can be nominated as a Supreme Court justice, although most justices are usually lawyers or judges. How would you recommend yourself as a suitable candidate?

Henry Aston

v

Bazaleel Wells & the
heirs and Representatives of
Arnold H. Dohrman dec.?

James W. McCulloch

vs

The State of Maryland &
John James, as well for the
State as for himself

opinion of this court, that the ac[t]
[en]titled "An act to impose a tax o[n]
[. . .] the State of Maryland (not [. . .]
[c]ontrary to the Constitution of the United States and void, and
[t]herefore that the said Court of Appeals of the State of Maryland
[e]rred in affirming the Judgment of the Baltimore County Court
in which Judgment was rendered against James W. McCulloch
[b]ut that the said Court of Appeals of Maryland ought to have
reversed the said Judgment of the said Baltimore County Court
and to have [. . .]
It is theref[ore . . .]
said Cou[rt . . .]
and the same is verily reversed and annulled — and this court
[P]roceeding to render such Judgment as the said Court of Appeals

THE POWER OF THE PEOPLE

The Supreme Court owes its power
to Chief Justice John Marshall.
The Constitution had not clearly
given the court the power to judge
laws passed by Congress, and the
court had not challenged any acts
of Congress until 1803. That year,
Marshall wrote the court's opinion
in the *Marbury v. Madison* ruling.
Marshall's judgment established the
Supreme Court's power of judicial
review. Since then, the court's role
has been partly to protect Americans
from government attempts to erode
the rights guaranteed to all citizens
by the Constitution.

Another landmark case under John Marshall, McCulloch v. Maryland (1819), established that the Constitution implied powers of the federal government without spelling them out, and that federal law takes precedence over state law.

Glossary

abortion: the deliberate termination of a human pregnancy

affirmative action: a system that deliberately favors those who are usually subject to discrimination

circuit courts: minor courts that cover a particular region

civil rights: the rights of citizens to political and social freedom and equality

conservative: holding traditional values and reluctant to change

damages: a sum of money awarded in compensation for a loss or injury

diplomats: officials representing a country abroad

discriminated: treated someone badly because of their sex, race, or religion

due process: fair treatment in the judicial system, including the right to a hearing in front of an impartial judge

estate: the money and property left by a person after his or her death

Jim Crow laws: laws that enforced racial discrimination in Southern states

libel: to publish a false statement that damages a person's reputation

nuclear option: a way for the US Senate to overturn the requirement for a minimum 60-vote decision to a simple majority of 51 votes.

polarized: divided into two completely opposing groups

segregation: the division of people on grounds such as race or gender

sued: began legal proceedings against someone

For More Information

Books

Linde, Barbara M. *Becoming a Supreme Court Justice.* Who's Your Candidate?: Choosing Government Leaders. New York: Gareth Stevens Publishing, 2016.

Peterson, Amanda. *Understanding Supreme Court Cases.* What's Up with Your Government? New York: PowerKids Press, 2018.

Torres, John A. *Desegregating Schools: Brown v. Board of Education.* US Supreme Court Landmark Cases. New York: Enslow Publishing Inc., 2017.

Websites

About the Supreme Court
www.supremecourt.gov/about/about.aspx
The official Supreme Court website, with links to detailed pages about how the court operates.

Landmark Cases
www.ducksters.com/history/us_government/landmark_supreme_court_cases.php
A list of historical cases in the Supreme Court that had a lasting impact on US law.

Index